John & Lesley,
with lov

CW00740184

Stories

By
Jackie Bartlett

Jackie Bartlett

First Published 2011 by Appin Press, an imprint of Countyvise Ltd
14 Appin Road, Birkenhead, CH41 9HH

British Library Cataloguing in Publication Data.
A catalogue record for this book is available from the British Library.

ISBN 978 1 906205 75 1

Acknowledgements

Many of these poems have appeared in *Envoi, Iota, Other Poetry, Obsessed with Pipework, Poetry Monthly, Poetry Nottingham, South* and *The Interpreter's House*. Some have been broadcast on BBC Radio Merseyside.

Out of Bounds is included in *Wirral, an anthology* published in 2002 as part of *Poet's England* series by Headland Publications, West Kirby, Wirral. ed. Gladys Mary Coles.

Going to Ludlow was a runner up in the *1992 Houseman Prize* , and *Hill 60, Ypres* was highly commended. Both appear in the Houseman Prize Anthology *A Sense of Place*

Mummies is included in *Making Worlds- One Hundred Contemporary Women Poets* published 2003 by Headland Publications in association with Second Light. eds: Gladys Mary Coles, Myra Schneider and Dilys Wood.

Contents

Grandchild

Fingers deep in shingle
she's delicately picking out
a trove of smooth stones and sea glass
head filled with stories
of mermaids and sea creatures

filling her bucket with treasure
running, sea- streaked, bronzed by summer
up the beach in red jelly-boots
to show and tell

and suddenly, another, long-ago beach
where you, red jersey loose over
frail bones and sea-cold flesh
spade cast aside, tin bucket freighted
with pebbles, sea-glass
shells and bladder wrack

step carefully towards us
intent on your sand-fort
on the sober task
of rebuilding the sea defences.

At the Window

Tide's out just now; there's only
mud-shine, bird-prints like runes,
remnants, reminders that something
was living here. Soon they'll be gone.

He never liked the curtains in this room.
Too busy, he said, too many shades of blue
competing with the sea, the sky.

They've searched for a week. Inshore craft
probing the mouths of coves. I've seen them
and the men, abseiling the cliff faces
from here to St. Govan's.

I got his clothes back today.
He'd left everything above the tidemark
so neat, so tidy: socks, boots, bar of chocolate
still wrapped. Blue shirt.

He tore that sleeve on a nail
sticking out of the shed door.
Caught it just above the elbow. Didn't
break the skin.

This is our room; mine now.
My room, my view, my blue curtains
my ancrene cell, my window on the world:

narrow sky, relentless surf, barren sea.
Such an empty, barren sea.

Timmy Phillips

First the banging of doors
shoes and boots ringing up the frozen yard
shouts cutting the frost-fast afternoon
like hot wire.

Then voices, confused, at the edge of panic
an echoing word, a half phrase:
"he's in t' pond" "He's goin' under, poor daft mutt."
"nowt to be done wi' 'im."

In summer the pond's edge green with reeds
and bulrush, brisk with life is our playground;
Irene, Pat, Derek and me
our Famous Four complete with dog-
complete with Timmy Phillips.
Now, midwinter's claimed it, turned it alien.

From behind trousered legs of dads
thick coats of mums and neighbours
we hear prophecies:

"..baker's horse and cart were lost in there years since..."
"...there's no bottom to it..."
"...they'll not get 'im out now, poor little beggar.."

Somebody slides a clothes prop across the ice
throws out a coil of rope;
a hopeful breath's indrawn...released
into a keening silence.

Finally we move off, all us gawpers
away from the dark
back to fire-lit kitchens
quieter now the hope's gone out of it.
"Just fancy, that poor daft dog.."

Over our heads cold stars are coming out;
one by one they are slowly coming out.

Tomatoes and Moira Shearer

Somebody's mended the door.
Your hand on the sneck remembers
to lift and turn, but the hinge that creaked
an early warning's gone; the old iron is oil-smooth
the door swings easily open.

Inside, your ears, cat-keen for sounds catch
a deep tomb-silence. You remember
lavender polish, the cosy shape of dolly-blue
the rag rug the cat peed on,
stew on the stove
the window with the broken latch.

You remember catkins on the cabinet, silver
cake boards for two bride's cakes
Mam at the table, purse flat as a pocket
totting up columns to make two bob last a week
see yourself at nine, 'on points' in your slippers
by the wire fire guard, practicing to be Moira Shearer.

You remember her in the garden
feet planted firm on the worn brick path
arms at full stretch
twisting tomatoes from trusses
laying them in your hands like a blessing.

Now the path leads you past the pear tree
they planted when your sister died, to where
rich earth, dark, mounded like a grave
clings to the last tomato vines. Crumbling to dust
their scent is already fading.

You cut a last sliver of green; crushed
in your hands its fragrance
will cling, linger on your skin, and scent it
on the long journey back.

Virtuoso

On my ninth birthday
you turned your ankle and fell
crossing Dovecote Lane.

Before that, I'd slipped
on the path newly laid with brick-ends
and clinker from a heap by the coal-shed door
and you told me off for being clumsy
dabbed at my split knee
with spit-on-a-rag and a slick of Zam-Buk
before kissing it better.

Watching you fall so elegantly
the skirt of your New Look coat
a blue pool around you
I saw, not gravel-burned hands
or shredded stockings sticky with blood
but a performance,
                    a demonstration
in the art of falling gracefully

and no different from your other accomplishments:
threading needles, rolling pastry, paring apples
so the skin fell from the blade
in thin ribbons of green.

Splinter

In the silence as the wind relents
there's the patient throb
of a tractor in the field
churning up nothing but stones.

It's the field where the woman lay down
pulled the grey blanket
of her grief over her head
became stone.

Her hands, they say, grew cold
as if frost replaced bone.
Touch them and you'd turn to rock
or ice and splinter
before you could turn away;

look into her bottomless eyes
and you'd run, stark mad
a loony, gibbering up the street
like Mad Johnny.

At the Hotel de Ville

Coming through the sunlit square
under dusty plane trees
whose shadow is a sprawl on the ground
the bride and groom
  -sugary and pink in the heat
   as melting figures on a bridal cake-

Maman, Papa, several fluttering sisters
done up like pretty butterflies;
pale brothers, nervous in stiff collars
big hands restless
without spanners and wrenches.

Now they pose for Etienne
below the tricolour, below window ledges
thick with flaming geraniums.

After the wedding in the dark-panelled room
they will emerge, blinking like bats.
Maman Premiere will wipe a tear, smile heroically;
Maman Dieuxieme will sniff
while Etienne clucks and shepherds
his brood for posterity.

Shuffle-footed and relieved
the Papas shake hands
breathe out last-minute cognacs
from beneath waist-coat buttons

and bridesmaids
pink and shiny as balloons
teeter on unaccustomed heels
damp inside their pink and shiny frocks.

Magpie

A flurry of dust and pecking
a gold eye rolling
then the bird lies slack
in his hands.

Clumsy with love
he splints sheened feathers
with flour paste
match-sticks and strips
torn from Mam's pudding cloths.

Across the table, Uncle Albert
who soon – not quite by accident –
will choke this wild creature with snuff, watches
from the edge of a light pool
plopping onto the table
from the overhead mantle.

Spreading, it touches
the boy's hair, deepens shadows
in the soft hollows of his neck.

Outside
beyond thin curtains
night is marking the window
with a black wing.

Street Music

Berlin November 1989

The opera-loving Scotsman
whose name I can't remember
but who took me once
to *The Magic Flute* at the Statopera
is dancing with Alma
along Kurfurstendamm
beneath street lamps heavy with light
to the music of the street-fiddler
who each day for forty years
has played outside the Blue Church
and to the music of the zither man who plays for coins
in the vacant lot on Kaiserplatz
where the synagogue stood.

Letter from The Silk Road

To my wife, loving greetings:

This comes to you by the hand
of one Thomaso, a silk trader
whose way lies by Bactra, Ecbatana
and, God willing, thus to Venice by summer.
He is owed 5 ducats for his pains.

God be thanked, a son! You, I pray are well;
safe, by Our Lady's grace
from the perils of childbed.
I yearn for your gentle company
and the comforts of home.

Yesterday, at first light we came
to Bukhara where we wait
for the Levantine envoy
who will conduct us to the Khan.

For now, we share our fires with travellers
whose talk is of the high passes where snow
gathers in drifts two cubits thick.

They speak also of ice towers
at whose heart is a blue as pure as the Holy Mother's cloak
and which sing, so they say, with the pure voice of a boy.

Such wonders! Yet our dreams
and waking hours are filled with deep dread.
We pray constantly:

Blessed Lady, let us not perish in unshriven wastes.

As I write
Maffeo is chivvying the muleteers
and tending the cook-fires.
Yesterday we slaughtered a hobbled mule
and so have fresh meat for our bellies.
For now, this, with our furs
is comfort enough.

We have travelled this far

in fur caps and capes, thankful also
for woollen stockings and drawers
        -though our skin is chafed
        with saddles and our own piss-

Our fine boots have proved too thin;
we bind our feet in mule skin.

Maffeo stinks like a bullock.

Forgive my crabbed script.
Cold bites deep and stiffens my joints.
Maffeo sends to you his brotherly salutations
and to our mother, his filial duty. Mine to her also.

Pray, reassure our investors
that all goes fairly with us.

Your husband,

Niccolo Polo

*Brothers Niccolo and Maffeo Polo undertook a trading expedition
To the court of Kublai Khan during which time Niccolo's son
Marco was born in 1254*

Going to Ludlow

Once we went to town which you had known
and where you'd lived with other loves.

It was a a winter day, growing dark
and the hills stood far off
stark as old confessors
holding secrets.

You drew me down tight streets
while your past flowed round us
like the looping river.

Your net, baited and cast
trawled me in, caught me
as gently in your mythology
as in the first embrace of our flesh.

And as willingly entered into.

Cuckoo

A small carved bird
inside a clock
calls you back each hour
from where you gather
cowslips, dog-violets
periwinkles and stitchwort.

We sit together
at the foot of the stairs;
you bound by shawls
into your wheeled chair.
I, bound by love to your side.

Your moth hands flutter
a "pat a cake";
I hear your familiar laughter
at *"the clever little mimic."*

Afterwards
sister-wife, beloved companion
you do not stay
but return to the hills
above Alfoxden

where we gathered apples
and wildflowers
before the fog came down.

*William Wordsworth's sister Dorothy suffered Alzheimer's
in the last years of her life but took pleasure from hearing
the cuckoo clock chime the hour at Rydal Mount.*

Hill 60 –Ypres

We have come up the track
from the road in the insect- noisy heat of noon
across the sad dust of horses and men
the grim rust of guns
to the rim of a green hill
where it rests against the sky.

At the top you walk on alone;
I rest on the edge of the hill's green bowl
watch you move away,
dispersing into points of light
pressing against the glare of a long day's heat.

Here trees, ancient yet new born
rooted in that long death
shake out their summer green.
In the long grass crickets
click like falling dice.

These are journeys we must make alone
to silent places where we learn the grief;
you to the monument, I to the place
where a tree stretches against the sky
and thunder speaks suddenly
like distant guns.

Stepping Out

Beachy Head was your way out.
Over the top, dramatic,
but hey that was the way you wanted it.
Why pretend you cared anything
for discretion.

Attention seeker;
how you must have craved
that exhilarating lurch
the final stepping- out, skirts a balloon.

And what a master-stroke to take a parasol
a flame of red silk
to light up the streaming air
like a stray sunspot.

I have to applaud
the sheer hey-look-at-me of it;
your single minded, spectacular intent.

Even when they fished you from the water
in a snaggle of whalebone and silk
you were smiling
as if you knew an amazing secret.

Pruning Dogwood

The leaves are back, glinting
rattling together like childhood pennies.

I have no heart for anything
other than looking; just admiring
the way they draw in the sun's last warmth
conduct it to the roots.

Last year we worked together she and I
pruning, stripping out dead growth
down to the rich red stalks.

Coppernob
the leaves are the colour your hair was once;
tongues of fire on ruby branches
or a burning bush.

Pentecost tree, her hands shaped you
as surely as they shaped me.

i.m. Sarah Margaret Swain 1915-2002

Seal Watching

Hauled-out seal
basking on flat black rocks
you are young
sleek in the ripple of muscle
beneath a marbled pelt;
a first-timer, out alone
on the wide shore of the world.

Oh, the pleasurable curl
and flex of your thick back flipper
switch-back genius
of the submarine state!

From under the brow of the cliff
under the flight path
of buzzards high on thermals
and lusts of spring
I watch you play in the sun-shiny
salt-tangy dazzle of morning

and resist the urge to follow
your dive through kelp forests
to feel the cool closing of water
over my head.

Maddonas at the Uffizi

Cats
in air-conditioned lairs
lie in wait
lurk in shadow
surprise us in our guilt.

They sniff us out
we, the unforgiven;
scent the blood
on our hands.

A dark glitter of eyes
stalks the rooms
follows us, snares us,
pinions us.

We are the prey;
there is no escape.

Memento

After Paschendaele
he kept a bent penny
in his pocket. Picked up
from the mud, it was bright

where the bullet had winged it
and shiny, the king's face
scarred to an idiot's leer.

He never said much; talked only
about how time, behind the lines
dragged itself along like a hobbled mule

or stopped suddenly
just as a bell pealed from a tower somewhere
or, in the real world
somebody got born, somebody laughed
caught a tram, lit a fag.

Ring

The ring I found
has a stone of glass
so clear and brilliant-cut
it could pass for a diamond.

I wear it my finger;
the one where the pulse beneath the skin
throbs straight to the heart.

The longer I wear it
the closer the fit
the more real it becomes.

And I like the look of it;
the glitter, the dazzle, the shine
that moment of radiance
when I lift my hand.

Rear View Mirror

I leave you at the roadside. You say
"Don't come any further, there's no need."
Through the rear view mirror I watch you heft
your leather travel bag, step carefully
through puddles to the high gates

and as if I were drowning, your life flashes
before my eyes. When the midwife laid you on me
face down, fierce with tears
and still so deeply joined
I thought the chain could never break.

Now, leaving you at the roadside
watching you walk away
I feel it prise apart, link by link by link.

This time a different pain;
no blood, no tears, only the rain
on the grass, drying.

Snow on Cheviot

The tups are on the hill behind the house
rooting among the beets, fleeces
at one with the mist of their breath
and the hot breath of calves
in hot sheds; with the smoke
of apple logs burning on hearths.

The land's assignation with cold
will be long; there's snow lying on Cheviot
and so, more to come before the winter's done
with us and we can breathe easy out of doors
not carry our breath in frozen clouds.

Even the trees, and pools where
frost is building its slow edifices
are still; mist and smoke move in quiet wreaths
across the field and crows in the white sky
weightless as charred paper.

And almost silence;
only the clanging of the cold metal gate
as I pass through, sounds across the hill
with the resonance of a struck bell.

Swans at Parkgate

Over there
the angular geometry of fields
is obscured by mist. The river
 a thin slick of steel.

Wind ruffles through sedges
with the sound of silver coin
clinking into my palm.

Below the wall
a boat lies upturned
its peeling keel the colour of sky.

Swans rise through the air
like notes of music through a scale;
their calls harsh, fierce as burning knives

a brazen, alien language
like that which you and I
could never share.

Watercolours

Rain. Wet on wet. An artist's composition.
You are standing at the water's edge
perfectly placed to draw my eye
towards a vanishing point
among the blur of hills.

I see where you have walked; your path
a bruise among the grass and sedges
and I follow you,
place my feet in your Wenceslas prints
to where the broad sleeve of river
narrows into the cut.

Your presence blesses me.

Upstream
the bell of a bone-rigged boat
shifting against the tide
sounds a knell in the quiet morning.

Further out
swans are rising and turning
against a soft palette of greys.

i.m. Horace (Sam) Swain. 1914-1993

Motor Bike Tree

For a whole summer
the motorbike lay
in a soup of black grease
outside the kitchen door.

He bought it for a tenner
from a mate at work
wheeled it home
along Queen's Road
past the bombed-out hotel
the wreck of Mona Street.

During the winter he dreamed
of trips to the Manifold Valley
seeing Surprise View in the early morning;
of speeding down the long roads
towards a line of hills
he could trace for us from memory.

Next summer, bike parts hung
-strange black fruit-
from the branches of the stunted apple tree
swinging gently, glossed with oil
like a starling's wing

while he,
mouth bristling curses
applied himself to other things.

For John and Liz.

Getting over it

Three months into your silence
I take your purple toothbrush
out of the bathroom
turn your photograph
 to the wall

and move the bed
to the other side of the room.
If you come back now
you won't find it.

The dressing gown
on the back of the door
the crumpled pyjamas under the pillow
that each night I fell asleep with
hanging on
to the scent of you

I'll give to the busker in the underpass
who plays air-guitar
-eyes manic
but whose voice is beautiful-

and after a while I might convince myself
that you have never been;
forget how you look
the feel of you, how
when you touched me
I felt, suddenly, real
totally visible.

Walking to the Clockmaker's House

When the photographs came out
the others said it wasn't you
third from the left on that ridge of rock
grinning, black hat pulled down
over your ears.

They said you were unfamiliar, swore
they couldn't place you, although
they remembered the walk, how it was so cold
it hurt to breathe during the climb; even
remembered the crazy rune trail
laid by birds across the track
but not you, they said. Were you really there?

Yet we'd all walked together before
you moved off, floundering through the drifts
in the shadow of the fir hedge
to find Alan. Backs to the track you'd peed
side by side into the snow.

And at the top, gasping and giggling
we'd all strung out on the ledge
above the Clockmaker's House
passed round hot cups, bread and apples
while you pulled your hat further down
and gurned for the camera.

The others can't recall you being there
that day. "No" they say, "that's not him.
Surely that's so-and-so.
Wasn't he the one in the black hat
who clowned around
made us laugh?"

The impression you made
has vanished from their memory
like our footprints on the hillside.
But I remember you; you were there.
You were there.

Starting Over

So here you are, back again
outside my door, waiting
as if you'd never left, never
just one day left, leaving the door
not closed but on the latch
as if, at any time you might reappear.

As if you had simply slipped out
for a loaf of bread in the way
Lotte told us her mother had
before she was picked up
off a street in their quiet little town
and sent somewhere nameless in the east.

Nothing much has happened in the time
you've been gone; I've puzzled and fretted
over your whereabouts
looked up and down streets and alleys
thought often of abandoning you.

Yet here you are, back again. Come in.
Be welcome. Let's start over.

Fever Ward – 1949

Kisses were delivered from a distance
with the sherbet lemons
clean nighties
and back copies of 'School Friend'.

Awake, beyond sleeping
moonlight a stone
on cold linoleum
and tucked-tight sheets
I wanted you. For only you

could cut off the head
of the nightmare crocodile
grinning and tick-tocking
towards me over the green floor.

Mummies

Each year
my granddad
slaughtered pigs

and hung the hams
and flitches
from the back kitchen rafters
above the oak-fuelled range.

He sat content
through the fugs of slow curings
while his skin
took on the colour of areca nuts
or Old Virginia.

His breeches
boots and shirt hardened
to a tanned carapace

his mouth became
the drawstring opening
In the purse of his face

his hands turned to leather
the veins slowly pumping
brine and ice water

mahogany juices
gathering beneath his fingernails.

He spent an age
slowly drying in silence

like the Inuit woman and her child
hacked from the permafrost
after six hundred years.

The King at Bosham

They are like blowflies, these courtiers
fat with flatteries
hovering at safe distance
as you pretend to study the breviary
and fret as the water darkens
your fine leather boots
and tunic of soft Sussex wool.

Floundering in soft shoes
they have shouldered your chair
to the edge of the water
sinking knee-deep in the bogs of Quay Meadow
while you railed
against the waste of an afternoon
more profitably spent tossing knucklebones
or recalling Sisyphus.

Finally, at dusk-fall, you hoik up your garments
wade knee-deep through reeds
remove your crown, toss it into the mud
where it rolls,
caught like a bowling hoop
in the oncoming tide.

*Henry of Huntingdon records that after Knut's encounter with the waves
he removed his crown and never wore it again.*

The Sitter

She spreads her rug
arranges, carefully, her draperies
and now turns the long white curve
of her back; a definitive statement
a demand for solitude.

He paints; she endures the ravishment
of his eyes, knows the way his skin burns.
He is unmarried but not innocent
of women; he craves the salty intimacies of flesh
and if he could, would rearrange her pose
have her half turn towards him
interpret the heavy hips, belly and breasts
the shadows and secrets of her body
in deep flesh tones.

She feels his ache, his desire
to trace each delicate bone in her spine
to unpin the coils of hair
watch it twist like a vine over shoulders
and half concealed breast.

He paints; beneath his brush subtle shades
of longing reveal themselves; pale flesh of thigh
rosy fold of groin, shadowy cleft above the tumbled
robe, the place his eye is drawn towards.

She breathes lightly wishing not to distract
with the slightest movement of muscle or skin.
Soon she will rise, abandon the props: alabaster jar
lengths of muslin, coarse red cloth, the sea shell
and leave; walk out into Kensington.

In her absence
he paints, draws the horizon
with a fine tipped brush
and around her vacated space
paints the sea.

Psamathe by Frederic, Lord Leighton(1830-1896)

Poor Tommy Shop

In his later years
my grandfather hoarded food.
Eating frugally at his niece's table
he secreted husks of bread, lumps
of cheese in the cupboard by his bed
stacking it neatly among shirts and underwear
tidy as a dry-stone wall.

He didn't eat it; kept it by him
a guard against the hunger of his youth
against the memory of walking
the slopes of saw-toothed fells
between Beckside and Lindale
arriving in the farm-wife's frowsty kitchen
before dawn for a bowl of porridge
too hot to eat before the farmer left

for the frost-rimed yard
clipping the ears of the hungry lads
dragging them, empty- bellied from the table
to haul clattering buckets
skimmed with ice
into hot sheds, among the breath
of milky calves;

against the memory of foraging
in the musty hen-house
for eggs, letting the slime of yolk and albumen
slide down his throat
from the blown shell.

*Poor Tommy Shop- A Lakeland expression for a workplace where food
was in short supply.*

Out of Bounds

Royal Liverpool Golf Club- Hoylake

The sky is bright today;
high cloud thins and separates
like cells. A wind from the east
flaps the flags on the greens
with a sound like whips cracking.

Sturdy in red
a golfer trudges the fairway
lugging his caddy-cart of woods
and irons. With no margin for error
he has overshot, sent the ball out of bounds
beyond the low turf wall of the seventh.

I too am out of bounds;
a trespasser among bunkers
and screening trees, slipping past The Stand
       - once the parade ring, with echoes
           of saddling bells, the gleam of silks-
skirting the edge of the links, crossing
the Royal Seventeenth, Lake, Field and Rushes
to reach the dunes

where wind lifts my hair
ruffles the water in the estuary
and the safe path to Little Eye
comes back in the slow turn of the tide.

I am here for Redwings, Fieldfares
Siskin, Snow Bunting, and, as night comes on
 the croak of Natterjacks
calling from the slack of the marsh
around Red Rocks.

Breaking Bread

Bare to his waist
braces adrift across bony hips
granddad washes at the deep stone sink.

Soap-blind and gilded,
a cherub in the evening sun
he shakes water from his hair
makes rainbows on scullery walls.

Then, in shirt fresh as a surplice
he comes to the table
cuts the bread, breaks open the warm crust
with the blade of the Goose Fair knife
set deep into its handle of yellowed bone.

White Linen

Each day she spreads her table
with a clean white cloth
laying it over a thickness
of iron-scorched wool.

Slowly circling
she smoothes its blank page
with rough fingers

perfects the surface
with tender strokes
caresses the crisp white cloth

remembering
cribs, marriage beds
winding sheets.

Bossa Nova Fox

Today I ask the neighbours
about the fox
who dances in the street
on his back legs
forepaws clasped as if overcome
by unexpected rapture.

The neighbours are cool:
                    been dancing
up and down the street for years
they say. *We ignore it.*

I watch from my window
from behind the blind.
A dancing fox is not easy to ignore
and this one's a master
of Latin American rhythm.

He can Rumba like a pro
Samba to perfection
but just watch him Bossa Nova:

he's on the beat, clicking and stamping
heels and toes twinkling
shimmying that sassy rear end
so the red fur glints
like a shower of sun spots.

Snowbound

It's possible to imagine
that below the snow line
folk are doing ordinary things:
settling bills, filling up four-wheel drives
doing the school run.

Up here it's silent.
Silent as that photograph
of Shackleton's doomed ship
everything buckling slowly
under the weight of ice.

Even our postman's gone to ground
like a fox in winter. No word is getting through.

I'm thinking of launching a balloon
from which to wave, or brushing up my Morse Code.
Even breaking out the semaphore flags:

Hello! We're here!

Imagine how beautiful they'll look
against the white.

Miss Carlin

This is the first time I've been summoned
to your room. Up steps so high
I can scarcely climb, tongue leaden
thick as pudding in my mouth

I follow you, your calves shapely in grey lisle
the heels of your sensible shoes
beating out a tattoo.

In your office you are magisterial; larger
than life. Your glasses glint sword blades.
You read out words for me to spell.

So is this it? Is this what it's all about?

Transformed, stammer left outside
I let words roll and fizz in my mouth
sweet as sherbet lemons.
I give them to you, a gift, perfectly wrapped.

At the door there's a tweak
of the satin ribbon tying up my hair.
Leaning down, you say
        "Well done, dear. Good girl."

Your words are my shield. I carry them
into the valley of the classroom
into the hollow silences of home.
At night I repeat them, quietly
like a benediction.

Wind at Southwold

Wind is a hammer at our backs
bowling a spindrift of picnic boxes
soda cans, a child's red shoe.

It's loosening the fixings on windbreaks
and deck-chairs. Grandpas are grasping
for toddlers and hats. Grandmas struggle
to keep skirts below the knicker line.

Everywhere's a racket of bluster and sound;
wind-tossed birds plough salt spray
surf booms over shingle, rattling back
with an artillery echo. Everyone is racing

for the shelter of the pepper-pot lighthouse.
In the lee of sugar-paste walls they cling together
-the spirit of Dunkirk – laughing and stoic
words wind-thieved from their mouths.

You sneak a kiss from my lips.
Later, in the stillness of our room
I will lick the salt from your skin.

The Summons

What are they doing
the people who, each night gather
under my window
to talk in hushed voices

speaking words that I barely understand
that sound like some strange dialect
from Friesland, partly recognised
as if I knew it, long ago.

I sit beside the window
on the other side of the wall
unseen by them, yet straining to hear
straining not to miss the secrets
they are trying to tell me

before they roar away in cars
which, like nightmare beasts, spin
their wheels, tossing up stones
that rattle against my window
like a summons.

Prints

Walking towards Little Eye
we follow Land Rover tracks, deep chevrons
slicing across rune prints of waders.

Strung out behind us, our own prints
are beads roped across a throat of sand.
Soon they will fill and vanish

leaving little trace of us; a contour
a fold in the sand, a trick of the light.

Above our heads, pink glitter
is printing the dawn across the estuary sky;
a wedge of grey-lags flying south
early sun on their under-wings.

Haiku for Spring

Raindrops in sunshine
among branches of white birch.
Spring's fibre-optic.

St Martin's Crypt

Ice on the line so the fast train is late arriving.
Already at the meeting place
you are hunched over the crossword
white-knuckled, gripping
a second cappuccino.

We do not kiss.
Instead I give you back the things
you left behind: soft shirt folded tight as a fist
cut-throat razor, the book you never read
on "How to Still the Monkey Mind".

More cappuccinos; in the fragrant fug
of the cafe our conversation is brittle:
a winter puddle's frozen surface.

We discuss the weather; touch upon
the trip to Sark we almost planned
for the summer; bury our long romance
beneath an edifice of small talk.

In the slow train going back
I think about your eyes: glinting like ice chips
blue and cold as this winter day.